THIS BOOK BELONGS TO :

_____

_____

All about me

Name: _____
Age: _____
Birthday: _____

Family: ♡
_____
_____

Pet:

Hobbies:
_____
_____

Favorite food:
_____

Favorite color:
_____

Best Friend:
_____
_____

Date __ / __ / __

I feel

1. Something that makes you unique.

Date __ / __ / __

I feel

2. Describe a "perfect day" that you recently had.

Date __ / __ / __

I feel

3. Write about your best friend.

Date__/__/__

I feel

4. Describe your happiest memory.

Date __ / __ / __   I feel

5. What is one thing you look forward to enjoying each day after school?

Date __/__/__

I feel

6. A favorite song you love.

Date__ / __ / __

I feel

7. The best thing that happened this week.

Date __/__/__

I feel

8. When was the last time you got into trouble?

Date __ / __ / __

I feel

9. What would you most like to learn over the next year?

Date __/__/__

I feel

10. If you could change one rule that your family has, what would you change?

_____
_____
_____
_____
_____
_____
_____
_____
_____

Date__/__/__

I feel

11. Write about a city you would like to visit someday?

Date__/__/__

I feel

12. If you found a Genie and he gave you three wishes, what would they be?

Date __ / __ / __

I feel

13. You are writing a letter to someone who is having a hard time making new friends at school. What do you write? What advice do you give them?

Date __ / __ / __

I feel

14. Do you have a piggy bank at home? How do you earn money to add to your savings?

Date__/__/__

I feel

15. What is the hardest thing about being a kid?

Date __ / __ / __

I feel

16. Write about a time you felt courageous.

Date__ / __ / __

I feel

17. What is your favorite holiday and why?

Date __ / __ / __

I feel

18. At what age is a person an adult? Why do you think so?

Date__/__/__

I feel

19. Something you use every single day.

Date __/__/__

I feel

20. What is something that makes your family special?

Date __ / __ / __

I feel

21. What is one lesson you learn from rude people?

Date __/__/__

I feel

22. If you could meet any fictional character from a book or movie, who would it be?

Date__ /__ /__

I feel

23. Do you find it easy to talk to people you don't know? What are some ways you can start up a conversation with someone you have never met before?

Date __/__/__

I feel

24. Explain how you help your family at home?

Date __ / __ / __

I feel

25. Favorite websites or apps you are grateful for.

Date __/__/__

I feel

26. Something that made you smile today.

Date __/__/__

I feel

27. Someone who inspires you.

Date __/__/__

I feel

28. A favorite place you like to visit.

Date __ / __ / __

I feel

29. Pretend you are a writer for your school's newspaper. Who would you like to interview for a news story and why?

Date__/__/__

I feel

30. Choose 3 people to say thank you to today.

Date __/__/__

I feel

31. If you had $1,000, what would you buy and why?

Date __ / __ / __

I feel

32. What do you like most about yourself?

Date __/__/__

I feel

33. Write a list of 5 things you can do to practice kindness to others.

Date__/__/__

I feel

34. Do you have any siblings? Think about what it might mean to be a good brother or sister and write about it.

Date__/__/__   I feel

35. Where is your favorite place in the world?

Date __/__/__

I feel

36. Something that was a wish come true.

_____

_____

_____

_____

_____

_____

_____

_____

Date __ / __ / __

I feel

37. What is your favorite movie? Write your review of the movie and why you think people should watch it.

Date __ / __ / __

I feel

38. Is there a homework subject you dread? Why do you not like getting homework in that subject?

Date __/__/__

I feel

39. What do you usually eat for breakfast every day? What, in your opinion, is the greatest breakfast food ever created? What makes it so great?

Date__/__/__

I feel

40. Are you a good friend? Why do you think so?

Date __ / __ / __

I feel

41. Write about a time you felt really happy. What happened? What made you feel happy?

Date __ / __ / __

I feel

42. If you could design a school uniform, what types of clothes would you suggest? What colors would they be?

Date __/__/__

I feel

43. What are you grateful for today and why?

Date __/__/__

I feel

44. What is a sport or activity you would like to try playing for the first time?

Date __/__/__   I feel

45. If you could give one gift to every single child in the world, what gift would you give?

Date__/__/__

I feel

46. Who is your favorite person on the planet?

What do you like most about that person?

Date __/__/__

I feel

47. A favorite food you enjoy.

Date __/__/__

I feel

48. What is something you look forward to doing the most when you are an adult?

Date __/__/__

I feel

49. What is your favorite thing about Mondays? Fridays? The Weekend?

Date__/__/__

I feel

50. What is a mistake you've made that turned out great?

Date __/__/__

I feel

51. What was the best part of your day?

Date __/__/__

I feel

52. Do you have pets? How do you take care of your pets? If you do not have a pet, what type of pet might you like?

Date __ / __ / __

I feel

53. Do you like to try new things? What is something new you have tried recently or would like to try?

Date__/__/__

I feel

54. What do you do when someone disagrees with your opinions? Is there a better way to handle conflicting opinions?

Date __ / __ / __

I feel

55. If you could travel back in time three years and visit your younger self, what advice would you give yourself?

Date__/__/__

I feel

56. If you were in charge of planning the school lunch menu, what foods would you serve each day?

Date __ / __ / __

I feel

57. Have you ever lost something that is important to you?

Date__/__/__

I feel

58. What is something you are afraid of? What helps you to feel less afraid of something?

Date __/__/__

I feel

59. Do you think it is important to keep your room clean? What do you like about having a clean room?

Date __/__/__

I feel

60. Who made you smile in the past 24 hours and why?

Date__/__/__

I feel

61. What are some of your favorite animals?

What do you like about them?

Date __/__/__

I feel

62. Describe your favorite location in your house and why you like it.

Date __ / __ / __

I feel

63. Write a story about a kid who is moving to a new school. How do you think they might feel?

Date __/__/__ I feel

64. What are 3 things you would need to be happy?

Date__/__/__

I feel

65. What five words do you think most describe you?

Date __/__/__

I feel

66. Something funny that made you laugh.

Date __/__/__

I feel

67. Have you ever forgotten to do your homework? What happened?

_____

_____

_____

_____

_____

_____

_____

_____

Date __/__/__

I feel

68. Write a letter to your future self in 20 years

Date __/__/__

I feel

69. Do you want to go to college? Why or why not?

Date__/__/__

I feel

70. What is your favorite part of your daily routine?

Date__/__/__

I feel

71. Do you like amusement parks? What are some of your favorite rides?

_____
_____
_____
_____
_____
_____
_____
_____

Date__/__/__

I feel

72. Have you ever been to the beach? Write about your favorite things to do. If you have never been to the beach, what would you like to do the first time you visit?

Date __/__/__

I feel

73. Currently, it is required by law that kids go to school. Do you think this is a good or bad idea?

Date __/__/__

I feel

74. What is something you like to practice so you can become better at it?

Date __/__/__

I feel

75. Look around the room and list all the items that you're grateful for.

Date__/__/__

I feel

76. Write about your favorite sport and why you like it so much.

Date __ / __ / __   I feel

77. Is there a favorite tv show you like to watch?
Write about your favorite character
and why they are your favorite.

Date __ / __ / __

I feel

78. What is something you learned today?

Date__/__/__

I feel

79. Imagine your parents are sending you away for a two-week summer camp trip. Would you be excited? Why or why not?

Date __/__/__

I feel

80. If you could be invisible for a day, what would you do?

Date __ / __ / __

I feel

81. Describe the last time someone helped you solve a problem at school.

Date __/__/__   I feel

82. Have you ever had to stand in line to wait a long time for something? What did you do while you waited? How did you feel while waiting? How did you feel once the wait was over?

Date__/__/__

I feel

83. What is one of the most important things you do each and every day?

Date__ / __ / __

I feel

84. Something that helps you relax.

Date __/__/__

I feel

85. When was a time that you felt lucky?

Date __/__/__

I feel

86. Is it a good idea to keep all secrets a secret?
    Write about examples of when it is okay to
    spill a secret and when it isn't

Date__/__/__

I feel

87. What is your favorite way to enjoy nature?
(i.e. walking in the woods, sitting on the
beach, or hiking in the mountains, etc.)

Date__/__/__

I feel

88. Who has forgiven you for a mistake you've made in the past?

Date __/__/__

I feel

89. Write an essay that starts with the line, "Tomorrow, I hope.."

Date__/__/__

I feel

90. What is the best gift you have ever given? Why was it so special?

Date __/__/__

I feel

91. A book you are grateful for reading

Date __/__/__

I feel

92. Something you are good at doing.

Date __ / __ / __

I feel

93. Write about someone who makes your life better.

Date __/__/__

I feel

94. Describe a weird family tradition that you love.

Date __/__/__

I feel

95. When was the last time you had a genuine belly laugh and why was it so funny?

_____

_____

_____

_____

_____

_____

_____

_____

Date __/__/__

I feel

96. What activity do you enjoy most when alone?

Date__/__/__

I feel

97. What activity do you enjoy when with others?

Date __/__/__

I feel

98. What body part or organ are you most
grateful for today? (e.g., your eyes
because you got to see a new movie)

Date __/__/__

I feel

99. What kind of clothes do you like to wear the most? What clothes do you not like to wear?

Date__/__/__

I feel

100. What do you think makes someone
a hero? Who are some of your heroes?

CPSIA information can be obtained
at www.ICGtesting.com
Printed in the USA
LVHW050930090121
675761LV00014B/532